Gabriel Justino

The resonances of a social project in the adolescent's existence

Gabriel Justino

The resonances of a social project in the adolescent's existence

An analysis of existential phenomenological psychology

ScienciaScripts

Imprint
Any brand names and product names mentioned in this book are subject to trademark, brand or patent protection and are trademarks or registered trademarks of their respective holders. The use of brand names, product names, common names, trade names, product descriptions etc. even without a particular marking in this work is in no way to be construed to mean that such names may be regarded as unrestricted in respect of trademark and brand protection legislation and could thus be used by anyone.

Cover image: www.ingimage.com

This book is a translation from the original published under ISBN 978-3-330-76760-7.

Publisher:
Sciencia Scripts
is a trademark of
Dodo Books Indian Ocean Ltd. and OmniScriptum S.R.L publishing group

120 High Road, East Finchley, London, N2 9ED, United Kingdom
Str. Armeneasca 28/1, office 1, Chisinau MD-2012, Republic of Moldova, Europe
Managing Directors: Ieva Konstantinova, Victoria Ursu
info@omniscriptum.com

Printed at: see last page
ISBN: 978-620-8-57675-2

ACKNOWLEDGEMENTS

I am extremely grateful to Professors Marlene Marchi de Sousa and Josefina Daniel Piccino for their lessons and, above all, for having broadened the horizons of my understanding of what it means to be a man in the world. Without this understanding, I wouldn't have progressed as far as I have in the sense of carrying out the mission I set out to achieve of minimising the excess of ignorance on this subject that has accompanied us men ever since we were thrown into the world.

I would like to thank the Sacred Heart University of Bauru, the professors Rinaldo Correr, Léa Sílvia Braga de Castro Sá and Sonia Maria Alves Paschoal.

I would like to thank my family Adriana and Nelson for everything and, above all, my mum Aparecida who gave me no other option but to study. I am eternally grateful.

Thank you to my fiancée, the woman who makes me a better person every day, for always believing in me, for the reciprocity and love that unites us, Thaiz Menezes.

I would also like to thank Novas Edições Acadêmicas, in the person of Iulia Ciumac, for their attention and helpfulness.

I'm also grateful to the unknowable mystery of life, the essence of which I'm not clear about, but which I somehow feel poetically in the beauty and contradiction of things.

NOTE OF CLARIFICATION.

The name "projovem adolescente", which appears throughout the book, is no longer used in the services that cater for adolescents, but rather "Serviço de Convivência e Fortalecimento de Vínculos" (SCFV). However, the structure of the SCFVs and their objectives have not undergone such significant changes; nevertheless, the term "Projovem" has remained throughout this book because it seeks to preserve the original text and the context in which the research was carried out.

This book is the presentation of a monograph presented to the Dean of Research and Postgraduate Studies as part of the prerequisites for obtaining the title of Specialist in Clinical Phenomenological-Existential Psychology, taught in partnership between Universidade Sagrado Coração (USC) and the Brazilian Society of Humanistic-Existential Psychology (SOBRAPHE), under the guidance of Prof. Ms. Marlene Marchi de Sousa and co-supervision of Prof. Ms. Josefina Daniel Piccino.

SUMMARY

CHAPTER 1	4
CHAPTER 2	7
CHAPTER 3	13
CHAPTER 4	23
CHAPTER 5	32
CHAPTER 6	39

CHAPTER 1

INTRODUCTION

Thinking about the existential aspects of adolescents' meanings in their relationship in and with the world is a concern that has accompanied the researcher since his adolescence, during his first experiences as a youth group leader at a religious institution he attended.

Subsequently, he worked as a psychology trainee with high school students at a state school, as well as working as a social educator at Projovem and other services at philanthropic institutions in partnership with the Bauru Welfare Department (SP, Brazil), which provide care for children, adolescents, the elderly and their families, for a period of four years.

Currently, in addition to his clinical work, the researcher works as a social psychologist in a support programme for low-income families, as well as developing training activities for social assistance professionals.

Recently, over a period of 1 year and 7 months, she coordinated a social project developed in a neighbourhood in the city of Bauru that catered for 222 participants aged between 3 and 17 and their families, one of the social assistance services of the basic network developed at the time being Projovem Adolescente.

Projovem Adolescente, now known as SCFV, is part of a social protection and promotion network of the Unified Social Assistance System (SUAS), operating, as it does throughout the country, in areas of social vulnerability, usually in partnership with philanthropic institutions or associations. The main aim of this activity is to provide a space for cultural, artistic, sporting and leisure activities, to develop potential for critical and proactive action in the world of work and in society as a whole, with a view to staying in school and strengthening family and community ties (BAURU, 2014).

The target audience is mostly young people whose families are beneficiaries of the Bolsa Família programme, but also young people at personal and social risk (15 to 17 years old). The themes developed in Projovem follow three main axes : social coexistence, the labour market and citizenship (BAURU, 2014).

Considering the proposals to help and protect adolescents, this study aims to understand the "resonances" that Projovem produces in the participants' existence, thus making it possible to highlight the scope of this project in building a more constructive and healthy existence.

Resonance is understood as the act of resonating, reverberating, reflecting, according to the Ferreira dictionary (2010), a term that originates in physics and is called the quality of what resonates.

In this context, the book presents research that seeks to understand the multiplicity of ways in which young people can be affected or touched by their experiences in the Projovem project and the possible consequences of these experiences for the way in which young people shape their own existence.

The aspects addressed by the researcher and the understanding of what the Projovem Adolescente Socio-Assistance Service consists of, serve to horizon the understanding and development of the current research, considering its phenomenological-hermeneutic qualitative direction in Heidegger in the theoretical discussion of the results.

According to Piccino (2013a), this way of making knowledge does not simply take place in the context of thematic choices, but opens up from "questions" of "what is researched" under the ground of understanding "what is" the Heideggerian thought of being man in and with the world, to the clarity of involvement as a method in this field of research.

This work was relevant to the researcher in terms of his own professional practice; the contributions to the science of psychology are related to descriptive, analytical, clinical, social and political practices, as it reaffirms the need for these projects to continue in order to improve the living conditions of adolescents.

The repercussions of the study for the adolescents are that the results provide knowledge of strategies to minimise the social and cultural vulnerabilities identified.

This book is presented in five parts, the first being the introduction, in which we explain the theme, objectives and justifications. The second part presents aspects of phenomenology based on Husserl's conceptions, as well as his view of man, method, philosophy and its developments, this being chapter two.

The third part presents a brief biography of Heidegger, emphasising the question of the meaning of being, the being of man as Dasein, the ontological constitution of care in Dasein, the existentials of Dasein, Heidegger's conception of the world and the facticity of

Dasein and its historicity, which is temporality, and is presented as chapter three.

The fourth part focuses on the methodology applied in the research, the researcher's procedures for collecting data, and the analyses, based on the method proposed by Amedeo Giorgi.

The fifth part discusses the phenomena identified in the research in the light of the Heideggerian understanding of existence.

The work ends with the sixth part reserved for the final considerations of the study, presented here in book form.

CHAPTER 2

THE UNIVERSE OF PHENOMENOLOGY

The phenomenological character of man in the world

The search for an understanding of a current of thought that neglects its historical, cultural and contextual aspects tends to lead to an analysis that is simplistic and doubtful as to its reliability.

Seeking to understand phenomenology is no different, as it is a complex task of understanding a series of historical aspects and paradigmatic crises in the forms of knowledge established in the relationship between man and the world up until Husserl, in order to obtain greater clarification of what man is like, how he apprehends the world and signifies it (PICCINO, 2012b).

Phenomenology opens up new horizons, providing a path to a new way of doing philosophy, science and thinking about culture, above all through a method that has no basis in natural science, but which, with rigour, can be the foundation for all knowledge (PICCINO, 2012c).

It's important to emphasise how, for Husserl, intentional consciousness is the original datum of any and all knowledge. It can never be deduced from subjectivity, in other words, the relationship between objectivity and subjectivity is inevitable.

Western Thought

As far as we know, since the emergence of man on Earth, changes in thinking and acting have taken place in the intrinsic and unchanging relationship with and in the world in the various fields of thought and knowledge: Philosophical, Scientific, Artistic, Theological, among others, and the history of thinking is already the history of man himself (PICCINO,2012b).

In the quest to succinctly understand what and how Western thought was formed, it is essential to refer to the whole culture, form of knowledge and way of thinking about life based on Greek conceptions (4th and 5th centuries BC), which spread throughout Europe and the regions colonised by Europeans afterwards (BELLO, 2004).

Bello (2004) also states that this way of experiencing the world waned in the Middle Ages, making a strong comeback in the Modern Age (15th and 16th centuries), especially with the study of the thinkers Plato and Aristotle, a period marked by the distinction between philosophy and religion, known as the Renaissance.

For Piccino (2012b), specifically in the 19th and 20th centuries, a radical change took place in the way of thinking about man's life in the world, mainly based on Husserl's phenomenology and Heidegger's Fundamental Ontology, in opposition to the positions defended by Western thought.

Dilthey's contributions and his proximity to Husserl in criticising Western Culture

Phenomenology was not the only tendency to go against Western thought in the mid-19th and 20th centuries. One important name in the line of these thinkers who went against Western thought was Wilhelm Dilthey (1833-1911).

For Husserl (2008), Dilthey was one of the greatest scientists of the Human Sciences or of the Spirit, dedicating his life to exploring the relationship between Nature and Spirit, as well as proposing an analytical descriptive psychology to complement psychophysical psychology.

The inductive experimental method of the natural sciences, which has taken hold of Western culture in science, philosophy and everyday thinking, neglects subjectivity or intersubjectivity in the researcher-researched relationship, compromising the search for truth through the rigour of a method (PICCINO, 2012c).

Still according to Piccino, empirical psychology and the human sciences have made a big mistake, using a method based on the natural sciences, thus defending the need for a methodology of its own for the human sciences, reasoning that is in line with Husserl (2008) and Dilthey (2001).

Dilthey (2001) states that, following the foundations of a "cause and effect" type of knowledge, as explanatory psychology aimed to do, we are surrounded by various hypotheses with no prospect of being proven by psychic facts. In his work, the author aimed for a human sciences project that was independent of the foundations that underpinned the natural sciences.

The origin of Phenomenology and its character of deconstruction

Talking about phenomenology makes it necessary to talk about Husserl's work and his search for solid foundations for knowledge. Piccino (2012c) believes that, in some way, with his phenomenology, Husserl participated in the deconstruction of Western mentality positions. Phenomenology is considered to have emerged and developed from Edmund Husserl.

Piccino (2012c) explains that Husserl was born in Prosznitz in Moravia in the second half of the ninth century, studied maths, physics, astronomy and philosophy and, influenced by Brentano's "descriptive psychology", developed the analytics of consciousness, thus founding phenomenology.

For Husserl (2008), science, like the whole of European culture, was in crisis, and this was the crisis of Western philosophy. Husserl understood that the intentions that drove the goals of doing science and people's everyday actions were in crisis.

For the phenomenologist, the whole of European culture, seen as a dominant culture in its time, had its historical roots in the beginnings of Ancient Greece, as already discussed by Bello (2004).

Husserl explains that this crisis, above all, was a methodological crisis of the European sciences which, in seeking to naturalise the Spirit, were based on natural-scientific foundations. For the author, the crisis was mitigated by the naivety of not considering the primacy of the Sciences of the Spirit in relation to the natural sciences, in other words, the non-existence of objectivity without subjectivity (HUSSERL, 2008).

For Husserl, the moral values that drove people's daily actions were in crisis. Phenomenology then presented itself as the possibility of a fundamental science, the mother of all sciences, to capture the fundamental essence of the spirit which, in this sense, could not be understood from a theological, mystical or religious perspective. In Husserl, this term refers to what is human, what refers to man; spirit is what moves men, ideas, human achievements, so saying sciences of the spirit is the same as human sciences.

According to Piccino (2012c) , with his phenomenology, Husserl made a major contribution to the philosophies of Heidegger, Sartre and Merleau Ponty, to the natural sciences and also to the human sciences, such as psychology, sociology and psychiatry, to name a few.

Man according to Phenomenology.

For Husserl, man is body, psyche (linked to reactive experiences) and spirit (reflective experiences). However, these three aspects are interdependent and cannot be understood separately (BELLO, 2004).

Husserl's phenomenology understands that man has a structure that is present in all men, a transcendental structure that makes it possible to know oneself and the other in an apprehension of the "essence" of things.

Bello (2004) explains that this structure is common to everyone, immanent to the subject. However, the contents experienced subjectively are different from person to person, as in the operations of remembering, fantasising, imagining and other experiences.

If a group of friends is told the memory of their first day at school, they will all know what has been said, considering the fact that they have also experienced the memory; however, the representation of the school that each one will have, as well as the idealisations of the first day at school, will be different.

This structure is only possible because of what makes knowing possible in the first place, which, according to Husserl, is the intentionality of consciousness. From intentionality, then, the phenomenologist develops a phenomenology or analysis of consciousness (PICCINO, 2012c).

Following Piccino, consciousness moves in a flow of experiences, operations in immanence also attributing meanings to the transcendent (exterior), always being conscious of and aware that it is consciousness, because the essence of consciousness is its ability to apprehend things and give them meaning.

Thus, consciousness is no longer understood as a place where data is stored. It is now seen as openness, the signification of things. In this way, consciousness and the external world are linked without the divisibility of object and subject, although subjectivity mediates the constitution of the world itself, as presented in Piccino (2012c).

Phenomenological method - (phenomenological reduction, eidetic reduction and rigorous description)

Defining what phenomenology is will always be a difficult and unfeasible task at various times, given the philosophical-cultural complexity it represents. In seeking to define it, we run the risk of fragmenting it. Here, we will briefly address quick positions towards a simple exploration of the phenomenological method in phenomenology and its extensions.

According to Goto (2008), since its birth in 1900, there have been several expansions in the philosophical horizon of phenomenology, making it difficult to find a simple definition that understands the scope of what it sets out to work on.

Bello (2006) approaches the meaning of the word phenomenology as the reflection of what is shown, making it possible to grasp its meaning, remembering that everything is shown to man as phenomena that have already been signified.

What is lived for man is, in fact, the work of consciousness in the world, and therein lies the inseparability of man and the world, a position radically defended by Husserl (GILES, 1975).

With the phenomenological method, by immediately grasping the meaning of things, we put everything we know about something in parentheses, thus performing the epoché, seeking to realise what positivism proposed to eliminate, that is, the essence, the eidos of things, but putting the world in parentheses means not forgetting that the conceptualisation of the world is given by consciousness itself (BELLO, 2004).

Phenomenology makes a great contribution to the various forms of knowledge by developing a method which, through phenomenological reduction (epoché), aims to describe a phenomenon as it appears, by means of eidetic reduction (essence).

Examples of developments in phenomenological methodology

Phenomenology, which originated with Husserl, didn't just remain in the mould and focus of its genitor. It spread to a number of lines of thought from the 20th century onwards, as mentioned above.

Max Scheler (1874-1928) devoted himself to questions of values, ethics, politics and religion. He studied and worked on topics in philosophy, the physical and natural sciences, economics, politics, geography and sociology. For him, the phenomenological method provided solidity and rigour to philosophical research, in an immediate search for objects of knowledge in general (GILES, 1975).

According to Scheler, phenomenology consisted of returning to things themselves through evidence, abandoning previous concepts, which were usually more linked to personal interests than to a love of the truth.

Another line of thought that stems from phenomenology is Existentialism, which, according to Piccino (2000b), is practically impossible to substantiate without phenomenology.

For Sartre (1970), one of the main characteristics of Existentialism, whether Christian or atheist, is the precedence of existence over essence, without determination, because man is thrown into the world and then becomes something; because, before becoming an existing entity, man is nothing, and the directives that guide men over things are given by men themselves, in a choice to signify what comes their way.

Heidegger's work is also an offshoot of phenomenology, but it will be explained more fully in the next chapter.

CHAPTER 3

EXISTENCE IN HEIDEGGER

Existence is a term that, in our daily lives, refers to things and objects in general. However, since Heidegger's work, it has taken on a different direction from what is normally understood in our Western culture.

Heidegger directs the word existence, specifically to man, by explaining who or how he is, through his fundamental ontology or analysis of dasein, exposing the prominence of man over all the other beings we know (PICCINO, 2012a).

Although authors such as Jasper, a German philosopher born in 1883, have worked on the subject of existence, no other philosopher seems to have gone as far as his contemporary Heidegger (HIRSCHBERGER, 1968).

This chapter will deal with some aspects of the Heideggerian conception of existence, serving as a backdrop for the discussion of the results obtained in the current study.

2.1 Heidegger's biographical history

Born in the town of Messkirch, in a region of the Black Forest in Germany in 1889, with a Catholic influence in his upbringing, as his father had strong ties to the Church, the thinker studied at a Jesuit school and lived with many Catholic people. As a young man, Martin Heidegger studied many aspects of philosophy that he would later question (PICCINO, 2012a).

Piccino says that Heidegger's life was dedicated to thinking. More than 60 years of his life were spent studying, writing and teaching, always guided by thinking. For 10 years, he replaced Husserl in Marburg teaching phenomenology.

With regard to Heidegger's links to Nazism, many accusations seem to seek to overshadow his entire oeuvre. In defence of the philosopher with whom he had contact for more than a decade, Medard Boss, a Swiss psychiatrist, states in the preface to his book "Zollikon Seminars":

> My reason, with all the baggage of psychiatric knowledge, told me that

> a man's social behaviour, including his political behaviour, does not necessarily diminish the genius of his thinking (HEIDEGGER, 2009, p.12).

In 1916, he received his doctorate and went on to publish and lecture extensively on subjects ranging from Greek to contemporary philosophy, as well as his Ontology. Heidegger died in Freiburg in 1976 (ABRÃO, 1999).

Using the phenomenological-hermeneutic method, in 1927 he published his best-known work, "Being and Time", in which he analysed existentialism (fundamental ontology).

For those who are interested in Heidegger's life, given the complexity of his life in terms of the influences of theology at first, philosophy, his involvement with Nazism, and what this regime was within the historical horizon that took place in Germany, a recommendation is the book "Martin Heidegger on the road to his biography" by Hugo Ott, professor of the History of Economics and the History of Sociology at the University of Freiburg.

The book cited here was only used as a source of reference in this study.

3.2 The question of the meaning of Being

If the aim of this chapter is to broaden the Heideggerian conception of existence, it becomes necessary to contextualise the question that Heidegger set out to investigate, opening it up to an understanding of what *Dasein* is and what "existence" is for the thinker from the Black Forest.

Heidegger (2012), in the first part of the first chapter of Being and Time, points to the need for philosophy to return to the question of what is,

According to him, it was a forgotten issue in his time, due to the fact that the knowledge that developed from Metaphysics thought it superfluous, unnecessary, and didn't make any effort to make it happen.

Piccino (2012a), discussing Metaphysics, presents it as the areas of philosophical knowledge responsible for investigating the being of entities.

Heidegger understood that, not only was it necessary to return to the question of being, which was unresolved by metaphysics because it was in obscurity, but it was also necessary to elaborate a question effectively, so that its direction would not be lost in its constitutive moments.

Piccino (2012a) explains that before Heidegger asked about the question of being, more specifically why metaphysics had abandoned the question of the meaning of being, it was necessary to find the entity par excellence capable of asking and thus presenting it in a hermeneutic phenomenology. This being par excellence, according to him, was Dasein.

Heidegger (2012), in the second part of chapter one of Being and Time, explains that, in the search for the meaning of being, it became necessary to develop what he calls fundamental analytics in the course of the book. In this, he sets out to present, to answer, what man is, what determines him as man and what his essence is.

Asking about the meaning of being obliged him to open up, to make visible the ways of being of the being he was asking about, in other words, the being Dasein.

In order not to run the risk of unclear exposition of some aspects of Heideggerian thought, it is understood that "being" is everything that we talk about, long for, speak about, think about, what and how we are. Being, on the other hand, refers to what reveals the being as it is, what makes it something and not something else, in other words, the essence of the being, as presented in the first part of Being and Timc (IIEIDEGGER, 2012).

Based on the aspects presented on fundamental analytics, which aims to present what Dasein is, it becomes necessary to discuss what man's existence is.

3.3 The human being as Dasein

In order to understand existence in Heidegger, it is necessary to focus on what it is to be Dasein, the differences between the entity Dasein in relation to other entities, as well as its determination, which takes place in relation to and with the world, as concluded in Piccino's (2012a) work on Heidegger's ontology (2012).

Considering the positions in the previous paragraph, it stands to reason that existing in Heidegger is a term exclusively directed at man, the only entity that exists, and it is understanding that exists, and this is different from all other entities that do not inhabit or form the world as man does, considering his entire ontological structure, which is yet to be discussed and expanded in this chapter and in the discussion of the results.

Piccino (2012a) explains that, unlike Dasein, other beings are called simply given or intra-worldly beings. Simply given or intra-worldly beings are those who, because they are not Dasein, do not inhabit the world like Dasein, because they are not world-formers, they affect, but they are not affective comprehension like man.

Heidegger (2009), in the Zollikon seminars of 23 November 1965, taking up questions relating to Dasein, differentiates between positions on the being of man, showing the thought of Freudian determinations, of Husserl's analysis of consciousness; to finally make an explanation of Dasein, placing it not just as a structure of man, but as that which constitutes him as such.

This makes it possible to affirm that within Heideggerian thought, Dasein is not a characteristic or something important in man, but rather the essence of man, what makes man man and not something else, another being.

3.4 The ontological constitution of care in Dasein

Broadening our understanding of Dasein, which, as we have already seen, is the essence of man, it is also understood that the essence of Dasein is healing, and healing, being cared for, in the sense of giving direction to Dasein's way of being-in-the-world, because it has no essence, as it is marked by an ontological indeterminacy (PICCINO, 2012a).

The ontological indeterminacy of Dasein concerns the aspect that nothing determines Dasein apart from its relationship with and in the world, because for it there is no essence, direction or conception prior to its being-in-the-world together and with, because its determination will be based on its relationship of intertwining with the world, in accordance with all the authors used in this research.

In any line of thought, scientific or philosophical, it is important to pay attention to the clarity of the terminology used. In relation to Heidegger's work, this is no different; on the contrary, the clarification of some terms becomes essential for a better understanding of his analytics, such as the terms: ontological and ontic.

Ontological refers to the constitution of the being of entities, the essence of a given entity, which also refers to the term ontology, which is an area of philosophy that seeks to know what an entity is, in other words, its essence. Ontic, on the other hand, points to the way real life happens, ways of being, based on facticity (PICCINO, 2012a).

Seeking to open up aspects of Dasein as a structure of care, it is important to emphasise that man is determined by being there in the world, together with beings that are not Dasein and with beings that are Dasein. Apart from this, man is nothing, he has no essence like the other beings in the world, also known as natural beings (PICCINO, 2012a).

Heidegger (2009), in Seminar II of the Zóllikon of 23 November 1965, states that Dasein does not have a determination like an entity of the natural sciences, but is an entity that is a being there in the world, and responds to everything that comes its way, taking care of being in its existence.

This dynamic, intrinsic to man in the world, is where and how man's existence occurs in Heideggerian thought. Understanding what existence is, in fact, consists of sticking to man in his daily life, without abstractions, but through a hermeneutic phenomenology that aims to bring to light the obscured nature of man in his being - there, together and with, Heidegger emphasises, because he is structurally "cared for".

It is Dasein's task to concern itself with simply given entities, which are entities in the hand and in the eye, and to concern itself with its own being and that of other Dasein, which are the forms of its existence, there in the world, in a dynamic that is always signified, because Dasein always directs its life, takes care of being, takes care of its existence (PICCINO, 2013b).

Based on Heidegger (2009) and Piccino (2012a), stating that Dasein takes care of its existence does not refer to moral care, but to ontological care, even if caring is a way of living a failed existence, or inadequate if thought of culturally, care here, ontological care, is not a constitution that is always present in Dasein, it is in fact what constitutes it as such.

Heidegger (2009), now in the Zóllikon seminars of 29 November 1961, makes it clear that numerous forms of presence meet Dasein, based on being open to the world, this occurring not only in sensorially perceptible modes of presence, but also as modes of memories, modes of hallucinated presence of something and even the absence of the presence of something, as in someone's mourning, Heidegger explains.

Dasein is care. Because care is its ontological constitution as an existing being, thus differentiating it from non-Dasein, non-world-forming beings, as presented so far.

For Heidegger (2009) in the Zóllikon seminars from 24 April to 4 May 1963, man is not an entity that is simply in the world; on the contrary, he relates according to his being by understanding it and other entities, whether they are Dasein or not.

Greater clarity as to the movement of Dasein in its being in the world through the fact of being cared for is possible from a better understanding of aspects relating to its structural, so-called existential, and ontological, since they concern all men, and are therefore also recognised as fundamental.

3.5 The existentials of Dasein

Having understood the question of the meaning of being, which led Heidegger to elaborate the analysis of Dasein or fundamental ontology, the basis for all other ontologies, it is possible to state that all the work started from a hermeneutic phenomenological view of what man is like.

Piccino (2012a) states that this analysis was based on observing what man is like in his daily life. This action was not focussed on an intuitive or abstract gaze, but on observing man's presence as it appears in his modes of being-there, dealing with the beings in his hands and eyes, and concerned with the beings that are Dasein.

It is understood that this dynamic of Dasein is possible because it is cared for through the fundamental structures, which are called existential, being structures of an ontological nature, present in all people and at all times, and cannot be seen as categories, classifications, but as what Dasein is in its being, emphasising once again the fact that Dasein is cared for.

So at this point, in order to better understand aspects of Heideggerian analytics , some existentials will be discussed briefly in this chapter.

In order to work on aspects of existential openness, we return to Heidegger (2009) in the Zóllikon seminars of 29 November 1961, already presented in this chapter, whose passage points to Dasein's openness to the world in all possible forms of presence, a dynamic made possible by the fact that Dasein is openness.

Based on this understanding, declaring that the entity *Dasein* ***is*** "openness" becomes the same as saying that the mere fact that the entity is in and with the world already makes it open to it, affecting and being affected, unlike other entities that are not open to the world.

Regarding the openness of Dasein, Heidegger clarifies...

> The state of man's openness to being is so important and determining for man's being that it constantly goes unnoticed thanks to its simplicity and imperceptibility, in favour of constructed psychological theories (HEIDEGGER, 2009, p.108).

This original "openness" is always in a relationship together and with, as well as being in contact with itself, in fact it consists of modes of relationship that are always meaningful. Since "openness" is the original existential, this means that *Dasein* is also "being able to be" already as an "understanding of being" and an "affective disposition". (PICCINO, 2013a).

Discussing the "power to be", Heidegger (2009), in the Zóllikon seminars from 24 April to 4 May 1963, points out that the "power to be" of dasein cannot be confused with mere possibilities: however, it is a "power to be" in the world, and this "power to be" is always historical.

This "being able to be" is not something that occurs merely through the action of the individual thought of as an entity trapped within itself with its own possibilities; on the contrary, it is a "being able to be" considering the historical situation of this entity, in a relationship with what is present, with what has already been and with what comes its way.

Piccino (2013b), addressing the existential "pre-understanding", points out that since Dasein is there, always in modes of relation, its way of being as it is, is in fact a constant "being" whose dynamics enable an "understanding of being", such an understanding only occurs and is only possible in the temporal horizon.

Still in Piccino, understanding the constitution of Dasein as care shows that, because it is originally "openness", it is at the same time "being able to be", "understanding" and "disposition to humour".

The existential mood of humour is also understood as affective tonalities and always concerns how Dasein responds to what touches it, in other words, by being "open", "able to be" and "understanding of being" - it responds to what it encounters from the world, as affective modes of daily dealing in being-there.

For the author, affective modes are completely linked to the "power to be" that occurs on each occasion and how she understands everything that it involves. I am affected in this or that way because I understand it that way and because the power to be that is at stake is this or that.

So far, we have explored some of the fundamental existentials of the being Dasein, considering that to be a man in the world is to be in relationship with everything that encounters him at all times, as we have already discussed, based on the emphasis on Dasein being cared for, so it is important, albeit briefly, to explain the structure of the existential being-in-the-world.

According to Piccino (2013a), "being-in-the-world" cannot be thought of in the same way as simply given beings are in the world, closed in on themselves, because Dasein not only occupies space in the world, but is also "open" to, affects and is affected at all times, and is also a world-former, considering the meanings of this world to which it is inseparably linked and in relation at all times.

Piccino (2000a), presenting the existential "being-in-the-world", states that Dasein, which is being in the world, always moves to occupy itself with, and concern itself with. This existential is possible considering the fact that Dasein is, can and understands being from the original existential "openness".

3.6 Heidegger's conception of the world

Returning to Piccino (2013a), it is important to briefly emphasise a fundamental concept of Heideggerian thought, which is the understanding of what the world is; because the world and space cannot be understood as physics had conceived them until then.

The author argues that the world is always a set of references, directions, norms, representations, what comes as a legacy of tradition, the world is not a place with various things together just occupying space, but a direction of meaning for, everything from the being that has primacy over all others, which is Dasein from the "openness" that is its nature, being there in and with the world.

Still according to Piccino (2013a), it is also fundamental to understand "temporality", which is also an existential aspect of *Dasein*, and is characterised as the essence of healing, since the being of Dasein is made up of modes of "temporality", which enables the being that is "understanding of being", to carry out such a movement in time, which is what enables the understanding or interpretation of being.

According to Piccino, temporality is a fundamental part of Heidegger's fundamental ontology, presenting it as the meaning of man's being.

3.7 The facticity of Dasein and its historicity, which is temporality

The question of Dasein being-there-in-the-world refers to a facticity that arises from its intertwining with the world through its historical reality, which is not really its own, but in the world, differentiating it from conceptions that until then understood man as an entity trapped within itself, separated from the world (HEIDEGGER, 2009).

Piccino (2013a) explains the term facticity within Heidegger's work as the everyday ways of being in the world, as they occur in human existence.

For Heidegger (2009), understanding what it is to be-there can only be done by leaving aside all the psychological, philosophical and other conceptions used until then, which presented man as an entity closed in on itself, endowed with some essence, categories such as: subject, person. This guides Heidegger himself at the beginning of the Zollikon Seminars.

Since man is determined by his relationship in the world and with everything that comes his way in a historical, spatial and temporal connection, from a Heideggerian perspective it is possible to say that this is where his existence takes place, in its facticity, under a historical horizon.

It is within this historical horizon that *Dasein*'s "power to be" takes place, as mentioned above when discussing the fundamental existential "power to be".

Returning to Heidegger (2009), again in the Zóllikon seminars from 24 April to 4

May 1963, this historicity discussed here is presented in the interdependence or, as Heidegger puts it, confrontation of what has been with what appears to meet it, so that Dasein can make up its mind.

Following Heidegger's reasoning on the question of historicity and/or temporality, Piccino (2013a) states that the past mediates Dasein's steps in the present, but that Dasein's being is always radically based on its future.

Still according to Piccino (2013), historicity cannot be confused with world history or universal history, because in fact this history is a consequence of the historicity of *Dasein*, which occurs in forms of "affective tonality", which, as has already been discussed, are presented as ways in which Dasein responds to the facticity of its daily existence.

Heidegger (2009), from Seminar IV of 5 November 1964, states that time is not simply the ticking of the clock, because time is not a sequence of nows as if aspects of the past as well as the future were separate from the now that we experience in the present.

Man is temporality and this is where his forms of relationship occur in his existence, observing an interdependence of past, present and future. Being in time or temporalising is history for Heidegger and is, in fact, existence (ABRÃO, 1999).

CHAPTER 4

THE METHODOLOGY APPLIED

This qualitative-phenomenological study aims to investigate the resonances that the Projovem Project produces in the existence of young people.

The choice of qualitative research and the phenomenological method was justified by the fact that this type of research provides a particular understanding of phenomena and an approach to the meanings and senses contained within them, with the results being analysed in the light of the Heideggerian understanding of existence.

The study involved six adolescents of both sexes aged between 15 and 17 who were members of the Projovem programme in the city of Bauru.

The testimonies were collected at a philanthropic institution in Bauru which, in partnership with the Welfare Department, runs the Projovem Adolescente Project. This service is a community centre for teenagers in a region with a high concentration of poverty, social vulnerability and few "cultural" resources. Its main objective is to promote family and community ties, based on the themes of: Social Coexistence, the Citizen Question and the World of Work.

The research, instrumentalised by the phenomenological method, followed the steps of Amedeu Giorgi's model (1985) through an interview subsidised by the following guiding question: ***"How is your experience in the Projovem Project?"***

Giorgi (apud Andrade and Holanda, 2010) was one of the pioneers in systematising the steps of the analytical procedures of empirical phenomenological research, based on testimonies about lived experience in relation to a particular subject that is the object of research.

During the testimony, the researcher made interventions and asked questions only when necessary to clarify doubts about the issue.

After collecting the statements, the first step was to transcribe them verbatim so that the researcher could access them in their entirety.

The second step was to make the text grammatically comprehensible, making only the necessary punctuations so that the speaker's speech didn't suffer any distortion of meaning and the written text was understandable.

Next, the method proposed by Amedeo Giorgi (1985) was used to phenomenologically analyse the testimonies. This author used four steps, which are detailed below:

1 - A global view of the testimony as a whole, in order to capture its meaning in relation to the object of the research.

2 - Division of the story into units of meaning.

3 - Transcription of Each Meaning Unit in Phenomenological Understanding.

4 - Composition of the Specific and General Syntheses, extracting the structure of what was experienced.

The specific synthesis is carried out for each particular statement, based on phenomenological understanding, consisting of a level of interpretation of what was experienced, which is already the result of the researcher's elaboration on the elements contained in the entirety of the statement itself.

The general synthesis consists of putting together the specific syntheses of all the testimonies collected in the study, in such a way as to compose a set of elements of the lived experience or invariants that make it possible to grasp its structure in relation to the subject studied, understood here as a phenomenon.

4.1 UNITS OF MEANING AND SPECIFIC SYNTHESES

In this topic we present the clippings of the Meaning Units (US), which refer to the excerpts from the statements that answer the guiding question: ***"How is your experience in the ProjovemT Project?"*** And then the specific synthesis, which refers to the researcher's experiential translation or phenomenological understanding of the phenomena contained in the statements.

All the names given to the participants are fictitious.

PARTICIPANT 1

DEBORA

15 years old, single, attending secondary school.

US: "Learning *more things...IT, but we don't remember much because we don't have many IT lessons. Ah, the teacher should teach more things, because it's not just football she has to teach, because if she's a PE teacher she has to teach more things. So she only teaches football, football to the boys and the girls sit in the corner and do nothing. It helped me to develop more patience with others, Ah... the person gets on your nerves, and if you don't like it you already think about hitting them in the face, but it's not like that, you have to think before you act, The help I've had here with my family, the respect that was difficult for me to have before, because I was very ignorant before, so it was the respect, the **help, these things, they marked me here at the Project***

SPECIFIC SYNTHESIS

Débora considers the project to be a space for learning, highlighting the insufficient number of computer classes to consolidate learning. She appreciates the sports and leisure activities, although she feels they are lacking and that football is prioritised for the boys. She recognises the project's contribution to her

development in terms of how they relate to people, their family and the respect and consideration they receive.

PARTICIPANT 2

ANNE

15 years old, single, attending secondary school.

US: *E'It's been the best experience, since I started the project, my life has changed, my behaviour with everyone, I'm much more polite, and it's changed my life, my way of speaking, thinking, acting... it's made me understand that we should never give up on any of our dreams, always trust in ourselves and get on with life, never stop, always walk with your head held high and work towards every goal, because those who dream can achieve them. If we don't chase our dreams, nobody will be able to do it, because it only depends on each individual. Projovem encouraged me never to abandon my studies, to be someone in life and if I hadn't joined the Project I wouldn't be studying, I wouldn't be thinking about going to university and I would be on drugs, practically I would have given up everything, my studies, my life and my family. Thanks to Projovem I'm a better person and I'm very proud to have done Projovem".*

SPECIFIC SYNTHESIS

Anne says that the Projovem experience has produced significant changes in her way of being in relation to herself and the world, altering her way of thinking and acting and strengthening her self-confidence in terms of realising her dreams. She has come to understand that her fulfilment depends on herself, that she values her studies, her family, avoiding drugs and improving her relationships with others.

PARTICIPANT 3

LAURA

17 years old, single, attending secondary school.

US: "... *I've learnt a lot from the people, from the coordinators, and everything I've been through here has been great for me going forward, like the things the teachers and the coordinator have taught me about STDs, about the environment, about the statute for children and adolescents. I also enjoyed the dance part with the teacher and the girls, because when we were going to perform it was so nerve-wracking, so we learnt to overcome this nervousness about going on stage and dancing, it's the same as when you're going for a job interview, that nervousness, that fear will pass right away, with dance we became more relaxed.*
The work I took part in on STDs was something I thought was really cool, it's something I want to do in my life, I found out about it through the project, as well as the dance, which I really enjoyed. My wish would be to become an STD lecturer and teach, pass on what I've learnt not just here at the project, because I want to have new experiences. I'm talking to an educator so that we can do it again, improve more".

SPECIFIC SYNTHESIS

Laura emphasises that Projovem has been an enriching experience for her life, in terms of learning and getting to know the people in the project, as well as issues related to health, the environment, rights and duties with the educational team. She emphasises her experience with dance, which helped her overcome emotional weaknesses. She feels grateful for the treatment she received in the project, which also helped her to communicate better and overcome difficulties in dealing with the public, as well as her desire to reproduce the knowledge she acquired about STDs.

PARTICIPANT 4

RICARDO

15 years old, single, attending primary school.

US: *Ah! It's been very good, but there are some people who make fun of people, swear at people, so it's a bit difficult to take part,...*
It's just that before I used to be on the streets fighting, doing things like that, so the project took me off the streets, now I'm in the project, no longer on the streets,... the project got me off the streets, because if I stayed there I'd be doing bad things.
Before I didn't do swimming, swimming showed me a lot of things, because I have bronchitis, swimming showed me a lot of ways, now I don't have bronchitis, I don't need to use medicine, the classes at the project are also very ***nice, good. So yesterday's "Educator X" class was very nice, the*** *clown* ***workshop*** *is very nice, before I used to just make fun of the others, I thought it was ugly, that the others were going to get screwed, then I thought no, it could be an* ***opportunity for me to do it and I enjoyed doing it, very nice".***
... before, I was a very aggressive kid, I used to swear at everything, I wanted to hit people, then the project opened up new paths for me, now I'm not like that anymore, now I've improved a lot.
... when I'm doing something wrong, I'll remember what the teachers said, I'll remember that".

SPECIFIC SYNTHESIS

Ricardo considers that his experiences at Projovem have been very good, despite the lack of co-operation and indiscipline of some participants who disrupt the activities. He recognises that the project has enabled him to spend less time on the streets and to distance himself from destructive possibilities, providing sporting activities such as swimming, which has improved his health, and artistic opportunities in the clown workshop. He believes that the project has opened up new avenues, enabling him to deal with his aggression better and develop more self-control in general. He says that the most important thing that will remain will be the good things he has learnt, the teachers' teachings about the wrong things he used to do.

PARTICIPANT 5

OTÁVIO

16 years old, single, attending secondary school.

US: *"For me it's been good, it's improved a lot, I hope it gets better and better, the students are developing, learning more things, it's been good. IT, sport, biology lessons, science, these things about technology, prejudices, these things that still exist in the world today and people talk about a lot, these things are developed in Projovem. In the computer class, they talked about first jobs, these things, I learnt a lot, it added a lot, a lot, how to do things and how to behave in an interview, dress appropriately, these things.*
The most memorable things I'll remember are the lessons I had here, my first job, the teachers, the games, all of it.
I wouldn't have a job today, I wouldn't know how to do an interview, I wouldn't have any education, I'd argue, fight, I'd become like those children who fight, get agitated, because today I don't act like that, but before I did. I was agitated, quarrelsome, very childish.
Improving the behaviour of the students a little, especially Projovem, improving people's behaviour, respect, education and the project would be better."

SPECIFIC SYNTHESIS

Otávio thinks that the project has been a great opportunity for him and the group to develop and learn in the areas of IT, sport, biology, science, technology and minimising prejudices. He points to the importance of computer classes in acquiring the information needed to enter the labour market. He emphasises the importance of recreational activities, leisure time and relationships with teachers. Believes that an improvement in student discipline, especially in the Projovem programme, would make the project better. He recognises that without Projovem he wouldn't be employed, he would still have childish experiences and his way of relating to people would still be inadequate and impulsive.

PARTICIPANT 6

ROBERTA

16 years old, single, attending secondary school.

US: *o Look, I think about it this way, if it wasn't for Projovem, not just the project here, but all the other Social Projects that exist here in the community, I could be on the street, messing around with things I shouldn't be messing around with, I could be a drug addict, a call girl, I think the project is good, the time I could be wasting on the street, and I'm learning new things here in the project, that's the good thing, not being on the street.*
After I joined the project, I learnt to reason a little more, because when I wasn't here I would explode at anything, it was very complicated, I couldn't say anything to myself and I would explode... before I didn't communicate with others, so I started communicating more and learning to calm my nerves, you know.
When it comes to teachers, you can't do anything they don't like and they start judging, they start saying things, but now when we do good things they can't see it, they only judge what we do wrong, what we do good they don't see.
I'll remember the friendships, the teachers, because like it or not they're friends, they're not just teachers, they're friends, but that's what I'll remember, the new things I've learnt, the teachers and the friendships I've made in the year I've been attending the project.
With IT I can get a job and I'll be able to handle the computer properly, with theatre I can do some courses there, do plays, with dance I can..., for example: Well! The girls here in the village want to set up a dance group, we already know a few things we've learnt in dance, so I think, who knows, maybe it will interact with my profession later on.
I'd like to say that regardless of what I've experienced here at the project, good or bad, I'd like to say that the project is a good thing, you know, and for me, if it were up to me, I'd bring a lot of people to do it, because at the project you learn a lot of things, I like going here?

SPECIFIC SYNTHESIS

Roberta emphasises that Projovem has provided a good environment with numerous activities and entertainment, encouraging her to think about the way she relates to people, curbing her nervousness and improving her communication skills.

She sees the Social Projects as an opportunity for new learning and redirection, without which she would possibly be involved in drugs, being a call girl or wasting time on the streets.

He emphasises the lack of understanding, impatience, demands, accusations and judgement of some teachers, who only take into account the wrong things done by the teenagers, not recognising the good things, such as the teenagers' involvement in the activities. She often feels that the teachers don't value, recognise or listen to the group. He points out that what remains most memorable are the memories of friendships, the positive bond with the teachers and the new things learnt.

She reveals that theatre, which was not part of her daily life, gave her the chance to learn how to make puppets and speak in public. She considers that she has also learnt new things in dance and IT classes, all of which she sees as opening up her professional possibilities. Regardless of the good or bad experiences, she sees the Project as good, different, a great learning environment, although she misses a lot, she likes going to it and if it were up to her she would bring other people to take part.

4.2 GENERAL OVERVIEW .

Unifying the specific summaries of all the participants made it possible to grasp the structure of what was experienced, which was shown in the invariant phenomena that emerged from the majority of the participants' statements. The idiosyncrasies in relation to the topic studied were also taken into account.

The testimonies revealed that the participants in this study conceive of Projovem as an environment that favours learning in the areas of health, the environment, citizenship, science, technology and IT, and is therefore an experience of personal growth.

IT appears to be very important to the young people, as a source of information and qualification for the labour market; however, one of the interviewees saw it as insufficient in terms of the number of lessons. Also noteworthy is the opportunity for young people to develop practices such as dance, art workshops, sports and playful experiences, fun, understood as a means of overcoming emotional fragility, and developing public speaking skills, improving health, interpersonal relationships, as well as being perceived as future job possibilities.

The prioritisation of football for boys to the detriment of other sports was pointed out by one of the teenage participants.

Most of the young participants emphasised the value of the relationships they experienced with their work team, and this appreciation is revealed through the feeling of gratitude they feel towards the team. Even when one of the interviewees pointed out the existence of some incomprehensible, impatient and unfair teachers, he managed to recognise and reflect on all the good things he had experienced with them. Projovem appears in the speeches of some of the interviewees as an important project because it brings contributions in the sense of increasing or rescuing the value of the family. The friendships established between the teenagers taking part in the project are

Despite the perception on the part of some, that the indiscipline of some participants hinders the progress of the group, preventing it from being better than it is. In the same way, the perception of the young participants is that Projovem enables or makes possible improvements in the affective sphere, favouring more satisfactory and healthy interpersonal relationships, helping adolescents to overcome aggressive and inappropriate actions, as well as acquiring greater self-control, thus improving relationships with people in general and with themselves.

They recognise the project as a means of avoiding drugs, prostitution, bad, destructive experiences and other possible evils.

In view of the benefits recognised, these young people see Projovem as an enriching space, generating possibilities for opening up new horizons, reconducting their own existence towards a more constructive path that makes it possible to build and carry out future projects.

CHAPTER 5

UNDERSTANDING AND DISCUSSING THE RESULTS

The insights gleaned from the testimonies of the participants in this study in relation to the resonances that the Projovem project produces in the adolescents' existence are understood here from the Heideggerian conception of existence. Therefore, in addition to Heidegger himself, all the authors referenced here share this existential perspective.

All the participants in the research felt they had benefited in some way from the Projovem Project, considering it a means of promoting learning in various areas of knowledge, personal growth, overcoming emotional difficulties and avoiding destructive experiences, as well as making it possible to open up new horizons on various levels of existence, according to clips from the participants' statements below:

> Débora considers the project to be a learning space and recognises its contribution to her development in terms of how she relates to people and her family.
>
> Anne says that the Projovem experience has produced significant changes in her way of being in relation to herself and the world, altering her way of thinking and acting and strengthening her self-confidence about realising her dreams.
>
> Laura Projovem has provided her with an enriching experience for her life, in terms of learning and socialising with the people in the project. She emphasises that the dance experience has helped her overcome emotional weaknesses. She feels grateful for the treatment she has received at the project, which has also enabled her to communicate better and overcome her difficulties in dealing with the public.
>
> Ricardo considers his experiences with Projovem to be very good, since it has enabled him to distance himself from destructive possibilities and has improved his health through sports. Projovem has enabled him to spend less time on the streets, to distance himself from destructive possibilities, providing sporting activities such as swimming, improving his health and giving him artistic opportunities in the clown workshop. He believes that the project has opened up new paths, enabling him to deal better with his aggression and develop more self-control in general.
>
> Otávio sees the project as a great opportunity to develop and learn for himself and the group in the areas of IT, sport, biology, science, technology and minimising prejudice. He recognises that without Projovem he wouldn't be employed, he would still have childish experiences and his way of relating to people would still be inadequate and impulsive.
>
> Roberta emphasises Projovem as an environment that offers countless activities and diversions, encouraging her to think about the way she relates to people, curbing her

> nervousness and improving her communication skills. She sees this project as an opportunity for new learning and redirection, without which she would possibly be involved in drugs, being a call girl or wasting time on the streets. She considers that she has also learnt new things in the dance and IT classes, all of which she sees as opening up her professional possibilities.

Heidegger (2009) in his seminars in Zóllikon from 8 to 16 March 1968, discussing the structures of man's being, more precisely the existential ones, points to a horizon for understanding the phenomena emerging from the participants' statements about the achievements of the Projovem Project.

These achievements related to learning, personal growth, overcoming emotional weaknesses, overcoming obstacles in various areas and opening up to new existential perspectives, are likely to happen on the level of everyday existence (ontic dimension) because structurally (ontologically) man is "original openness".

According to Heidegger (2009), "openness" is an original (ontological) existential that reveals how an entity is not closed in on itself, enclosed in a psychic interiority. On the contrary, its relational dynamics, at all times, take place in modes of being together with the "simply given entities", which are the things, situations, activities and knowledge with which it relates. The "entities simply given" are "intramundane", that is, they are in the world, but they are devoid of the world, because they are not openings of meaning. World, here understood as a structure of meaning, a context of language, of signification that is always historically in movement.

Dasein ***is*** "worldly", cooriginating with the "world", linked in a relationship of interdependence, in which one does not exist without the other, in other words, there is no man without the world and no world without man, therefore they cooriginate. In this relational context, man (Dasein), in addition to simply given beings, also relates to other Dasein, which are other men and his own *Dasein*, which is the relationship established with himself. This reveals that *Dasein* (man) is always already an *Eom-relation".* It is in this being-in-the-world with others that meaning is given as the unveiling of the beings that come to it.

For Heidegger (2009), to be *Dasein*, which is the essence of the human being, is to be open to the world that abruptly comes to meet you, and *Dasein* is always a response to this encounter, because it is independent of a will. This response simply takes place in the relationship between man and the world, occurring in the most diverse ways, in modes of being-there, that is, of existing.

Being-there underpins the possibility of experiencing and signifying what we encounter in a multiplicity of ways.

According to Piccino (2013b), the established mode of attachment includes intimacy, the most personal and subjective way of being and this mode is revealed in and through contact; this implies that man in his daily life is all the time showing his world, showing how he attaches himself, how he signifies what comes his way. This author explains that affectivity is the possibility of "being ***by"***, founded on in being open to and experiencing the world in the unfolding of everyday life in a variety of ways.

In this way, it was possible to grasp, through the testimonies of the young people taking part in the project, the different ways of bonding established with the experiences lived in the context of Projovem, revealing a multiplicity of ways of giving affectivity. The particular and unique way in which each person is touched, affected and their ways of responding, made it possible to grasp the meaning and sense given by them to this experience and the resonances it is producing in their lives. It was observed that, in some way, all the participants were positively affected by the Projovem Project. The modes of affectivity were revealed in the participants' way of being and relating to their realities in the changes they are producing in their lives. They were touched and affected in a unique way in terms of personal development, learning, changes in behaviour, overcoming difficulties and weaknesses, enriching their own world and broadening their existential horizons.

Drawing on Heidegger (2009) when he refers specifically to affections, he clarifies that man, being Dasein, is structurally disposed to humour, in other words, he always is in some way, affects and is affected by what challenges him in his existence, thus Heidegger speaks of a pleasurable power-being-affine.

In this sense, we understand that Projovem adolescents are not simply affected by the project, but their affections are closely linked to what challenges and summons them.

Heidegger (2009), in his seminars in Zollikon from 24 April to 4 May 1963, presents another existential that reveals the possibilities of learning and growth for the participants in the current research: ***"being able",*** which reveals the fluid movement of existence.

"Being able to be" is possible because *Dasein* is originally "openness". "Being able to be" is already being "understanding of being" and "disposition of humour". This movement of Dasein highlights the fact that man always affects and is affected in his being-there-in-the-world, understanding himself and the world in its totality of (being) things (PICCINO, 2013a).

In this sense, the participants' accounts reveal that the relationships established in the Pro-Youth Project have enabled the expansion of various possibilities, increasing the construction of a more satisfying and enriching existence on the various levels of their existence. "Being able to be" as one of the structural aspects of man (ontological) is shown in the daily existence (ontic) of each young person, in their growth, in their learning, in overcoming difficulties, in their dreams and in the opening up of their possibilities and broadening of their existential horizon.

Being-in-the-world is also an existential of Dasein, in its ontological structure, possible through original openness, along with the other existentials, as already shown by Piccino (2000a) and Piccino (2013a). It shows that it is in the relationship with the world that each person has become what they already are and are, in this relationship that they become what they are not yet - this is the fluidity of existence.

Casanova (2006), also addressing the affectations of the relationship between being-there-in-the-world, in line with Piccino (2012a), clarifies Dasein's significations not as being properties, or originating from itself; however, the multiple significations originate from the relationships established in the everydayness of the world, in other words, in the mundanity of the world.

The adolescents' readings and/or interpretations of the Project's resonance in their existence do not come from themselves; this affectation and signification occurs in the movement of the adolescent's inseparability from the horizon of reference, the adolescent always being a relation and determined by the relations in this historical horizon (world), as Heidegger (2009) guides.

Another phenomenon that emerged from the testimonies was the adolescents' appreciation of relationships with staff, participants and themselves, in positive feelings such as gratitude, recognition, more satisfying and healthy relationships, all of these phenomena based on affective bonds, which helped to minimise tempers and reduce aggressive and inappropriate attitudes among adolescents, which led to an improvement in relationships with themselves, with others in general and in family relationships.

The emergence of these phenomena can be seen in the clipped expressions of the participants below:

> Roberta feels encouraged to think about the way she relates to people, curbing her nervousness and improving her communication. Despite the lack of understanding on the part of some teachers, she points out that what remains most memorable are the memories of friendships, the positive bond with teachers and the new things learnt.
>
> Otávio emphasises the importance of play and leisure activities and the relationship with teachers.
>
> Ricardo Believes that the project has opened up new avenues, enabling him to deal with his aggression better and to develop more self-control in general. He says that the most important thing that will remain will be the good things he has learnt, the teachers' teachings about the wrong things he used to do.
>
> Laura emphasises that Projovem has been an enriching experience for her life, in terms of learning and living with the people in the project.
>
> Anne opens herself up to the realisation that her fulfilment depends on herself, that she values her studies, her family, avoiding drugs and improving her relationships with others.
>
> Débora Recognises the project's contribution to her development in terms of the way she relates to people, her family and the respect and consideration she receives.

Based on the phenomena that emerged from the testimonies, it is possible to move on in this discussion towards apprehending and understanding aspects related to the importance of the relationships developed in the project, with entities (things, ideas) and with people (Dasein) on the part of the adolescents.

Based on Piccino (2013a), it is once again pertinent to point out that the adolescent's relationships will always already be in a singular form of response, regardless of whether these relationships are with things, objects, ideas or people, because the adolescent, being Dasein, is a relationship and a response to everything at all times.

Following the Heideggerian idea of existence, adolescents have no prior essence, their essence is being in relation, always needing references so that they can be-there in some way, considering their power-to-be in and with the world (CASANOVA, 2006).

Projovem, as a space for referrals and educational cultural references for adolescents from the basic Social Assistance Network, focusing on attention and care for families in a context of marginalisation and poverty, is of great value in the development of its actions, understood here as positive affectations, because it mediates relationships that launch adolescents towards horizons of valuing family relationships, themselves and people in general, as well as contributing to future prospects and diverse cultural expansion.

With regard to the phenomena that emerged in the relationship between the adolescents and the work team, there was a feeling of gratitude towards the team, an improvement in the relationships between the participants and in family ties, with the project becoming a space for enriching and more satisfying existential opportunities.

Since Dasein is structurally a relationship, at all times, in the various ways of being with things and with people, the adolescents' relationships with the work team are identified in ways of disagreement, incomprehension, impatience and injustice on the part of some educators towards them, this phenomenon revealing precisely the multiplicity of ways in which Dasein can respond (PICCINO, 2013b).

The positive, negative and all possible forms of affectation discussed here in the experiences of adolescents in the Projovem programme occur in modes of response due to the fact that adolescents (Dasein), structurally speaking, are also affective in their relationships.

> At every moment when being-there is, it is already from a possible way of finding itself. These possible ways always refer, in turn, to affective tonalities that radically refine the existential space of openness and permeate the very coexistence between being-there in general (CASANOVA, 2006, p55).

The project affects the adolescent just as everything affects them, because it is a relationship and a response, enabling meanings on an ontic level (singular of their existence) and in the same way it is also an affectation.

> Heidegger says: "the peculiar situation of Dasein's existence is to always be directing its life, to always be in the situation of having to

> take care of being". Animals, trees, clouds, avocados, stones, etc., do not have to take care of being, they simply are, they are there where they are (HEIDEGGER, 2009 quoted by PICCINO, 2013a, p.4).

Taking into account the importance of adolescents' relationships in and with Projovem for their existence, and the relevance of this issue within the Heideggerian conception of existence, the resonances learnt from the results of the current research reveal the importance of guiding actions for adolescents that serve as a reference in their existential apprehension of life in the world, because without the world there is no Dasein, there is no existence, man and the world are not distinguishable, they become inseparable.

CHAPTER 6

FINAL CONSIDERATIONS

The results achieved in this research show that the proposed objectives have been achieved, to the extent that the Projovem project (SCFV) has produced visible positive resonances in the existence of young people, contributing greatly to a more satisfactory and healthier direction in the various planes of their existence, minimising the possibilities of social marginalisation, considering the cultural context in which they are inserted and the objectives of the basic assistance policy implemented in the services for living together and strengthening bonds.

In addition to the clarity achieved about the benefits of the project in the lives of young people, the relevance of this study is also evident in the contribution made to the science of psychology with a hermeneutic phenomenological research based on the Heideggerian perspective, in which the discussion moves between the ontological and the ontic, opening up new perceptions and understandings about ways of being and existing.

For psychologists, it brings the possibility of learning about a way of understanding and analysing existential phenomena, as well as political and social contributions, in terms of recognising and valuing public policies that meet society's needs to combat violence, marginalisation and increase projects and services that bring prospects for the development of healthier and more constructive existences, thus contributing to a society in which people have more dignity, more prospects and more opportunities to fulfil themselves in the various existential dimensions.

This work opens up the possibility of developing other research with new horizons to be investigated, such as the evaluation of other social projects with other perspectives or optics.

The results obtained are relevant because this is a public opinion survey, which, given the importance of its results, can be extended to future surveys to assess the effectiveness of other community centres.

In the municipality of Bauru in 2017, the basic protection network of Social Assistance aims to serve various families with Services to Strengthen Links for children and adolescents aged 03 to 17, as well as centres for the elderly and intergenerational, corresponding to 03 to 59 years, all of which are spread across various territories of the municipality, mostly neighbourhoods with a high concentration of poverty, social vulnerability and few information and educational resources (BAURU, 2017).

As a researcher, this work was a watershed in existential terms, given the professional contributions made by someone who had never familiarised himself with the explanatory psychologies studied in undergraduate school, and who found in existential phenomenology a way forward when he sought to see the phenomena overshadowed by the pre-understandings apprehended in and with the world, thus understanding that it is better to seek to see things rather than explain them. In the words of Fernando Pessoa.

> It's not enough to open the window
> To see the fields and the river.
> It's not enough not to be blind
> To see the trees and flowers.
> You also need to have no philosophy at all.
> With philosophy there are no trees: there are only ideas.
> There's only one closed window and the whole world outside;
> And a dream of what you could see if you opened the window, which is never what you see when you open the window (Alberto Caeiro)

REFERENCES.

ABRAO, B. S. Os Pensadores: História da Filosofia, São Paulo- SP, Nova Cultura, 1999.

ANDRADE, C. C and HOLANDA. A. F. Apontamentos sobre pesquisa qualitativa e pesquisa empírico-fenomenológica, Estudos de Psicologia, Campinas, 2010. Available at: < http://www.scielo.br/pdf/estpsi/v27n2/a13v27n2.pdf> Accessed on: 16/03/2015.

BAURU. Municipal Department of Social Welfare. Coexistence and bond strengthening service for adolescents and young people - Projovem Adolescente. Bauru, 2014.

BAURU. Municipal Department of Social Welfare. Normative Standard for the Basic Social Protection Network - Coexistence and Bond Strengthening Service, Bauru, 2017. Available at: < http://www.bauru.sp.gov.br/arquivos2/arquivos_site/sec_bemestar/padroes_normativos/Rede%20de%20Prote%C3%A7%C3%A3o%20Social%20B%C3%A1sica/PN%20Serv.%20Conviv%C3%AAncia%20e%20Fortalecim.%20de%20V%C3%ADnculos%202017.pdf> Accessed: 28/04/2017.

BELLO, A. A. Phenomenology and the human sciences: psychology, history and religion. Bauru, SP: Edusc, 2004.

____________ . Introduction to phenomenology. Bauru, SP: Edusc, 2006.

CASANOVA. M A. Nothing on the way: impersonality, nihilism and technique in the work of Martin Heidegger. Rio de Janeiro: Forense Universitária, 2006.

DILTHEY, W. Ideas on a descriptive and analytical psychology. Rio de Janeiro: Via Verita, 2011.

FERREIRA, A. B H. Mini Aurélio: O dicionário da língua portuguesa/ Aurélio, Curitiba: Positivo, 8ª Ed, 2010.

GILES, T. R. History of Existentialism and Phenomenology. São Paulo: Ed da Universidade de São Paulo, 1975.

GIORGI, A. A Sketch of Psychological Phenomenogical Method. Phenomenology and Psychological Research. Pittsburg: Duquesne University Press, 1985.

GOTO, T. A. Introduction to Phenomenological Psychology: Edmund Husserl's new psychology. São Paulo: Paulus, 2008.

HEIDEGGER, M. Seminário de Zollikon, Petrópolis: Vozes; Bragança Paulista: Ed Universitária São Francisco, 2009.

HEIDEGGER, M. Being and Time. Editora da Unicamp; Petrópolis RJ: Editora Vozes, 2012.

HIRSCHBERGER, J. História da Filosofia Contemporânea. São Paulo: Editora Heder 1968.

HUSSERL, E. The Crisis of European Humanity and Philosophy. University of Beira Interior, Covilhã, 2008. Available at: <http: //www.conteudojuridico.com. br/pdf/cj035380.pdf> Accessed on: 23/06/2013.

PICCINO, D. J. Specialisation course in Existential Phenomenological Clinical Psychology: Aspects of Martin Heidegger's Ontology of Facticity. Bauru-SP, USC-Sobraphe, 2012a.33p. Handout.

____________ . Specialisation course in Existential Phenomenological Clinical Psychology: Birth context and characteristics of the Western mentality. Bauru-SP, USC-Sobraphe, 2012b. 21p. Handout.

____________ . Training course in Existential phenomenological psychology and analysis of the existential relationship - Are: Involvement as a method. São Paulo, SOBRAPHE, 2013a. 13p. Handout.

______________ . Specialisation course in Existential Phenomenological Clinical Psychology: Husserl's Phenomenology, USC- SOBRAPHE, 2012c. 16p. Handout.

______________ . Training course in phenomenological psychology
Existential and analysis of the existential relationship: Pathology and Existence, Psychopathology and Existence Existential Interpretation of Borderline Stages, SOBRAPHE, 2013b. 24p. Handout.

______________ . Specialisation course in Existential Phenomenological Clinical Psychology: On Method. Bauru-SP, USC-SOBRAPHE, 2012d. 9 p. Handout.

______________ . Meeting of phenomenology and analysis of existence, 2000, São Bernardo dos Campo SP[Paper presented]. SOBRAPHE FENPEC/UMESP, 2000a.

______________ . What is existentialism: existentialism- phenomenology- humanism. In: ______________ Phenomenology and the Analysis of Existing. São Paulo: Methodist University of São Paulo, SOBRAPHE, 2000b. p. 65 - 74.
SARTRE, P. J. Existentialism is a Humanism. Les Éditins Nage, Paris, 1970. Available at: < https://mail.google.com/mail/u/0/?shva= 1#inbox> Accessed on: 25/05/2013.

REFERENCES CONSULTED:

FEIJOO, A M. A existência para além do sujeito: a crise da subjetividade moderna e suas repercussões para a possibilidade de uma clínica psicológica com fundamentos psicológicos-existenciais, Rio de Janeiro: Via Verita, 2011. .
OTT, H. Martin Heidegger on the road to his biography. Lisbon: Instituto Piaget, 2000.

PESSOA, F. Poemas completos de Alberto Caeiro. São Paulo: Laluzi Editora, 2007.

More Books!
yes

MIX
Papier aus verantwortungsvollen Quellen
Paper from responsible sources
FSC® C105338

Printed by Books on Demand GmbH, Norderstedt / Germany